To Sadie-cakes
from Mimi & Papa
Christmas 2012

Whisper and Shout

Whisper and Shout

Shout

Poems to
Memorize

Edited by
Patrice Vecchione

Cricket Books
Chicago

Seventh printing, 2009

Library of Congress Cataloging-in-Publication Data

Whisper and shout : poems to memorize / edited by Patrice Vecchione.—
1st ed.
    p. cm.
Summary: A collection of poems on different subjects and in different
styles, that lend themselves to memorization.
Includes bibliographical references and index.
  ISBN 0-8126-2656-7 (alk. paper)
  1. Children's poetry, American. 2. Children's poetry, English. [1.
American poetry—Collections. 2. English poetry—Collections.] I.
Vecchione, Patrice.
  PS586.3 .W48 2002
  811.008'09282--dc21

                                                    2002000591

In memory of my mother,

Peggy Vecchione,

and all the knowing by heart

Contents

Acknowledgments

Many thanks for their team effort at Cricket Books to Marc Aronson, Judy O'Malley, and Carol Saller; also to Louise Brueggemann. Charlotte Raymond has my gratitude. Dear friend Diana Wertz, the Gault School librarian, shared the store of poems to memorize that she has collected, some of which appear in this book. Thanks to Alyssa Raymond for her help once again. To my project assistant Marion Silverbear, thanks for both heart and humor. Over the past twenty-plus years of teaching poetry in schools, students have shared with me what they know by heart, including most recently Mrs. Julian's class at Robert Down School in Pacific Grove. The reference librarians at Monterey Public Library have certainly memorized this face, and never run from my questions!

Introduction

Some of my best friends are poems, and maybe that's true
for you. If not, some of these poems may become good
friends as you turn the pages of this book. Reciting poems
on the walk to school seems to shorten the distance.
When you are lonely, a poem can give you company.
During the boring times or when you're sick in bed with
the flu, poems will remind you that there's more to life
than just this. If you are afraid of the dark, a poem may
soothe you. Its melody and rhythm can help slow the racing
pulse back down again. If you meet somebody that you
like, poems can be a present to give.

There are poems you will want to possess after you've
read them once. When you find a special poem, you want
to have it forever. It may speak to you about something
you've never thought of before. Maybe it startled you or
made you laugh. A poem can remind you of somebody. If
you read a poem about a grandmother, it may get you

thinking about your grandma who lives hundreds of miles away. Saying the poem isn't the same as being with her, but it will make her feel closer. Poems can live in our thoughts, roll on our tongues, rest in our hearts, or set our feet to tapping. You may find yourself repeating the words all day long, chanting the poem into your memory.

Memorizing Poems

What things do you know by heart? I asked some students that question, and here are a few of their answers: my phone number and other important phone numbers, like my mom's and dad's cell and work numbers, and 911; the Pledge of Allegiance; my screen name and computer password; our zip code; song lyrics; piano scores; how the sky looks on cloudy and sunny days. We remember these things because we either need to keep them at hand or because we want to revisit them whenever we choose.

The things that we commit to memory we know differently than the things we don't. The way to really know a poem, to befriend it, is to learn it by heart. Then, it's yours for always. You can take it wherever you go, and don't have to worry about losing the paper it was written on. To remember a poem you have to really read it, notice its details, the sounds it makes in your mouth, where it takes you in your imagination. Through memorizing poems you develop your ability to observe and remember the details of life.

The poems then influence who you are and who you will become. A memorized poem can become a star to wish upon, or a way to say thanks, or a question you're not sure you want the answer for.

There are some poems you feel you have to share, to say them out loud and make them sing for real. To your friend on the school bus, you say, "Do you want to hear a poem?" Or it just sounds so great, you even tell it to your basset hound! (My three cats have been a good audience for more than one new poem I've just fallen for.) There are other poems that are quiet and private; you'll want to say them in your smallest voice, to hold them inside.

When I discover a poem I want to know by memory, I read it over and over again to myself and aloud. Sometimes, I make associations between an image or idea in the poem and something I already know well. For example, when, as a child, I learned Carl Sandburg's poem "Fog," I would imagine my own cat walking. When I first read "The Word Woman" by Patricia Hubbell, I saw a picture of an older woman who was part angel and part sage. Seeing that picture in my mind helped me to remember.

Rhyme can help your memory, too. Even if you can't remember the exact word that ends a line, you may recall that its sound is similar to that of the word at the end of the line before.

But rhyming poems are hardly the only ones to memorize. All poems have the elements of sound at work in them; that's partly what makes them poems. We begin learning the patterns of sound that are present in poetry as babies. Poems are made out of everyday language that's given special attention. They are unique presentations made of words (the meaning and sound) and of lines (the way the words appear on the page).

Each poem has a rhythm that's its own, if not a drum-banging kind of rhythm, at least a pattern of sound. Think of your heartbeat: it may be fast or slow, regular or irregular, but the come-and-go, the ba-bum, is a pattern.

Some poems are written in meter—the words in the lines are arranged systematically and are stressed in particular patterns. Some poems repeat words, phrases, or entire lines to create a rhythm. Many contemporary poems are written in what is called free verse. They don't rhyme, but they still have rhythm. It's just not rhythm that's as predictable as regular meter and rhyme. When you read a poem, listening for different kinds of sounds, from brisk and galloping to steady and solemn, from expected to surprising, will help you recall how it goes.

Start with a small poem, savoring each image, line by line, then stanza by stanza, and repeat each part a few times, till it's yours. Memorizing a poem can take awhile. But, it's sort of like eating sunflower seeds—easy to begin, hard to stop!

In addition to poems to remember and recite by yourself, you'll find some of the poems in this collection are fun to recite with friends and classmates. When I say "maggie and milly and molly and may" by E. E. Cummings out loud, my mouth gets to feeling full of those m and m's, and a group reciting this poem makes it all the more m-marvelous.

Listen to the sounds in that one. The silly rhymes in "Dinky" by Theodore Roethke make it really fun to perform. Paul Fleischman's poem "Dusk" is meant to be read by two voices. Get a friend and try saying it out loud together, trading lines. You might wear some costumes and put some of these poems on stage.

Kinds of Poems and Poets

In *Whisper and Shout* you'll find loud poems like the book's first selection, by Gwendolyn Brooks, "Speech to the Young: Speech to the Progress-Toward." It seems to insist on being said out loud. And quiet ones like Marjorie Agosín's "My Mother's Eyes." Many of the poems are playful and silly like Gelett Burgess's poem "My Feet." Ogden Nash also makes us laugh with his poem about a germ. And beware: you may never taste soup quite the way you did before, once you've read Lewis Carroll's "Beautiful Soup"! The poem with the fastest pace, though hardly the shortest, in this collection, is May Swenson's "Analysis of Baseball." "It's about the ball, the bat, the mitt, the bases. . . ." Just try saying that one slowly!

When you say some poems aloud, you feel them jangling in your bones. Cynthia Zarin's poem, "Song," will twist your tongue a bit, as will "Weather," whatever the weather is like outside while you're reading its delightful plays on a word and an idea. Robert Frost's images in "The Road Not Taken" will unfurl like the road itself. Other poems seem like a voice singing, and there are those that put a tear in your eye. Some may cause you to want to shout back at them. And then there are those you simply want to keep in your heart for a rainy day.

Most of the poems in *Whisper and Shout* were written by authors whose names appear beneath the poems. The brief biographies at the back of the book will tell you a bit about these poets. Many of them are contemporary authors, while others lived long ago. You'll also find work here by authors who are unknown, or "anonymous." The term literally means "unknown name." Some anonymous poems belong to ancient societies and began as oral poetry. Others may be listed as anonymous because the author of the poem didn't feel safe claiming it. If the poet's work was not in agreement with those in power, it could have been dangerous to identify himself with the poem. Or, perhaps somebody at a later time didn't believe that the person whose name was on the poem had written it. This was sometimes the case with poems written by women during periods in history when women were not considered capable of writing poems, or it wasn't thought proper for women to do so.

Some of the poems included are called "traditional." These poems are the ones that may have been recited many, many years ago and handed down from generation to generation. A traditional poem or song may not have just one set of words, but there may be variations to it, due to many retellings. Think of a story you've told someone. That person passes on the story to someone else, and so on. When you hear it again, it's almost the same story— but not quite. The snake that you described may have grown in length, the cold of the night is now freezing. Have you ever played the game Telephone? In stories, songs, and poems that come from oral traditions, memory works in the same way.

There are also poems that don't have individual authors because the cultures that produced them felt that the poems were the possession of the entire tribe, not the creation of any one person. As with the Cherokee poem included here, many voices contributed to and shaped the poems as they were retold over many years.

The humorous and light verse in *Whisper and Shout* includes limericks and riddles. Limericks are nonsensical and silly verses with a regular singsong meter and rhyme that makes them easy to remember and fun to recite. We're not sure where the term originated, though it may be from the town by that name in Ireland. Riddles are an ancient form of literature. The earliest recorded English riddles are from a very long time ago—the eighth century. A riddle is a word puzzle, often phrased as a question, for the reader to figure out.

The Poetry Habit

Pick your favorite poems from this collection, and give them away, or keep them tucked safe in your heart and mind. But don't stop there. Keep hunting for new gems to add to your collection. Then within you, always, you'll have a treasure trove of new and distant places, the sound of rain water, your mother's eyes, comfort in an unfamiliar place, immediate celebrations: You'll have poems to tickle or soothe, to prod, to whisper and shout. And with them you can talk back to the world where you live, voicing the verses you love.

Patrice Vecchione

Whisper and Shout

Come through the Door

(Poems about Life)

Speech to the Young: Speech to the Progress-Toward

(Among them Nora and Henry III)

Say to them,
say to the down-keepers,
the sun-slappers,
the self-soilers,
the harmony-hushers,
"Even if you are not ready for day
it cannot always be night."
You will be right.
For that is the hard home-run.
Live not for the battles won.
Live not for the-end-of-the-song.
Live in the along.

Gwendolyn Brooks

5

I Hear America Singing

I hear America singing, the varied carols I hear,
Those of mechanics, each one singing his as it should
    be blithe and strong,
The carpenter singing his as he measures his plank
    or beam,
The mason singing his as he makes ready for work,
    or leaves off work;
The boatman singing what belongs to him in his boat,
    the deckhand singing on the steamboat deck,
The shoemaker singing as he sits on his bench,
    the hatter singing as he stands,
The wood-cutter's song, the ploughboy's, on his way in
    the morning, or at noon intermission, or at sundown,
The delicious singing of the mother, or of the young
    wife at work, or of the girl sewing or washing,
Each singing what belongs to him or her, and to none
    else,
The day what belongs to the day—at night the party
    of young fellows, robust, friendly,
Singing with open mouths, their strong melodious
    songs.

Walt Whitman

from **Macbeth,** *Act V, Scene 5*

To-morrow, and to-morrow, and to-morrow,
Creeps in this petty pace from day to day,
To the last syllable of recorded time;
And all our yesterdays have lighted fools
The way to dusty death. Out, out, brief candle!
Life's but a walking shadow, a poor player
That struts and frets his hour upon the stage
And then is heard no more: it is a tale
Told by an idiot, full of sound and fury,
Signifying nothing.

William Shakespeare

■ Dream Deferred
■
■ What happens to a dream deferred?

Does it dry up
like a raisin in the sun?
Or fester like a sore—
And then run?
Does it stink like rotten meat?
Or crust and sugar over—
like a syrupy sweet?

Maybe it just sags
like a heavy load.

Or does it explode?

Langston Hughes

Song

My heart, my dove, my snail, my sail, my
   milktooth, shadow, sparrow, fingernail,
      flower-cat and blossom-hedge, mandrake

root now put to bed, moonshell, sea-swell,
   manatee, emerald shining back at me,
      nutmeg, quince, tea leaf and bone, zither,

cymbal, xylophone: paper, scissors, then
   there's stone—Who doesn't come through the door
      to get home?

Cynthia Zarin

■ Recuerdo
■
■
We were very tired, we were very merry—
We had gone back and forth all night on the ferry.
It was bare and bright, and smelled like a stable—
But we looked into a fire, we leaned across a table,
We lay on a hill-top underneath the moon;
And the whistles kept blowing, and the dawn came soon.

We were very tired, we were very merry—
We had gone back and forth all night on the ferry;
And you ate an apple, and I ate a pear,
From a dozen of each we had bought somewhere:
And the sky went wan, and the wind came cold,
And the sun rose dripping, a bucketful of gold.

We were very tired, we were very merry,

We had gone back and forth all night on the ferry.

We hailed, "Good morrow, mother!" to a shawl-covered
  head,

And bought a morning paper, which neither of us read;

And she wept, "God bless you!" for the apples and pears,

And we gave her all our money but our subway fares.

Edna St. Vincent Millay

"Recuerdo" = Spanish for "I remember."

■ Shiloh
■
■ A Requiem (April, 1862)

Skimming lightly, wheeling still,
　　The swallows fly low
Over the field in clouded days,
　　The forest-field of Shiloh—
Over the field where April rain
Solaced the parched ones stretched in pain
Through the pause of night
That followed the Sunday fight
　　Around the church of Shiloh—
The church so lone, the log-built one,
That echoed to many a parting groan
　　　And natural prayer
　　Of dying foemen mingled there—
Foemen at morn, but friends at eve—
　　Fame or country least their care:
(What like a bullet can undeceive!)

But now they lie low,
While over them the swallows skim,
And all is hushed at Shiloh.
There is ruin and decay
In the House on the Hill:
They are all gone away,
There is nothing more to say.

Herman Melville

■ The Road Not Taken
■
■

Two roads diverged in a yellow wood,
And sorry I could not travel both
And be one traveler, long I stood
And looked down one as far as I could
To where it bent in the undergrowth;

Then took the other, as just as fair,
And having perhaps the better claim,
Because it was grassy and wanted wear;
Though as for that, the passing there
Had worn them really about the same,

And both that morning equally lay
In leaves no step had trodden black.
Oh, I kept the first for another day!
Yet knowing how way leads on to way,
I doubted if I should ever come back.

I shall be telling this with a sigh

Somewhere ages and ages hence:

Two roads diverged in a wood, and I—

I took the one less traveled by,

And that has made all the difference.

Robert Frost

I'm a Rumble of Jumbles

(Wordplay Poems)

"I saw Esau sawing wood"

I saw Esau sawing wood,
And Esau saw I saw him;
Though Esau saw I saw him saw,
Still Esau went on sawing.

Anonymous

A Word

A word is dead
When it is said,
   Some say.

I say it just
Begins to live
   That day.

Emily Dickinson

■ Weather

■
■

Whether the weather be fine
Or whether the weather be not,
Whether the weather be cold
Or whether the weather be hot,
We'll weather the weather
Whatever the weather,
Whether we like it or not.

Anonymous

Beautiful Soup

Beautiful Soup, so rich and green,

Waiting in a hot tureen!

Who for such dainties would not stoop?

Soup of the evening, beautiful Soup!

Soup of the evening, beautiful Soup!

   Beau—ootiful Soo—oop!

   Beau—ootiful Soo—oop!

Soo—oop of the e—e—evening,

   Beautiful, beautiful Soup!

Beautiful Soup! Who cares for fish,

Game, or any other dish?

Who would not give all else for two p—

  ennyworth only of beautiful Soup?

Pennyworth only of beautiful Soup?

   Beau—ootiful Sooo—oop !

   Beau—ootiful Sooo—oop !

Soo—oop of the e—e—evening,

   Beau-ti-ful, beauti—FUL SOUP!

Lewis Carroll

Player Piano

My stick fingers click with a snicker
And, chuckling, they knuckle the keys;
Light-footed, my steel feelers flicker
And pluck from these keys melodies.

My paper can caper; abandon
Is broadcast by dint of my din,
And no man or band has a hand in
The tones I turn on from within.

At times I'm a jumble of rumbles,
At others I'm light like the moon,
But never my numb plunker fumbles,
Misstrums me, or tries a new tune.

John Updike

in Just-

in Just-
spring   when the world is mud-
luscious the little
lame balloonman

whistles   far   and wee

and eddieandbill come
running from marbles and
piracies and it's
spring

when the world is puddle-wonderful

the queer
old balloonman whistles
far   and   wee
and bettyandisbel come dancing

from hop-scotch and jump-rope and

■ it's
■ spring
■ and
the

goat-footed

balloonman   whistles
far
and
wee

E. E. Cummings

Analysis of Baseball

It's about
the ball,
the bat,
and the mitt.
Ball hits
bat, or it
hits mitt.
Bat doesn't
hit ball, bat
meets it.
Ball bounces
off bat, flies
air, or thuds
ground (dud)
or it fits mitt.

Bat waits
for ball
to mate.
Ball hates
to take bat's

bait. Ball
flirts, bat's
late, don't
keep the date.
Ball goes in
(twack) to mitt,
and goes out
(twack) back
to mitt.

Ball fits
mitt, but
not all the time.
Sometimes
ball gets hit
(pow) when bat
meets it,
and sails
to a place
where mitt
has to quit
in disgrace.

That's about
the bases
loaded,
about 40,000
fans exploded.

It's about
the ball,
the bat,
the mitt,
the bases
and the fans.
It's done
on a diamond,
and for fun.
It's about
home, and it's
about run.

May Swenson

■ Jabberwocky

'Twas brillig, and the slithy toves
  Did gyre and gimble in the wabe;
All mimsy were the borogoves,
  And the mome raths outgrabe.

"Beware the Jabberwock, my son!
  The jaws that bite, the claws that catch!
Beware the Jubjub bird, and shun
  The frumious Bandersnatch!"

He took his vorpal sword in hand:
  Long time the manxome foe he sought—
So rested he by the Tumtum tree,
  And stood awhile in thought.

And, as in uffish thought he stood,
  The Jabberwock, with eyes of flame,
Came whiffling through the tulgey wood,
  And burbled as it came!

One, two! One, two! And through and through
    The vorpal blade went snicker-snack!
He left it dead, and with its head
    He went galumphing back.

"And, hast thou slain the Jabberwock?
    Come to my arms, my beamish boy!
O frabjous day! Callooh! Callay!"
    He chortled in his joy.

'Twas brillig, and the slithy toves
    Did gyre and gimble in the wabe;
All mimsy were the borogoves,
    And the mome raths outgrabe.

Lewis Carroll

■ Tapping
■
■ **(for Baby Laurence, and other tap dancers)**

When i pat this floor
   with my tap

when i slide on air
   and fill this horn intimate with
the rhythm of my two drums

    when i cross   kick
scissor   locomotive

   take four for nothing
four we're gone

when the solidarity of my yoruba turns
join these vibrato feet
   in a Johnny Hodges lick
a chorus of insistent Charlie Parker riffs

when i stretch out for a chromatic split
together with my double X
   converging in a quartet of circles

when i dance my spine in a slouch
   slur my lyrics in a heel slide
arch these insteps in free time

   when i drop my knees
when i fold my hands
   when i decorate this atmosphere
with a Lester Young leap and

   enclose my hip like snake repetitions
in a chanting proverb
   of the freeze

i'm gonna spotlight my boogie
   in a Coltrane yelp

■
■
■ echo my push in a Coleman Hawkins whine

i'm gonna frog my hunch in a Duke Ellington strut

quarter stroke my rattle
    like an Albert Ayler cry

i'm gonna accent my march in a Satchmo pitch

    triple my grind in a Ma Rainey blues

i'm gonna steal no steps
    i'm gonna pay my dues

i'm gonna   1   2   3

    and let the people in the Apple
go hmmmp   hmmmmp   hmmmmmp

Jayne Cortez

Like a You or a Me

(Poems of Family and Friends)

Knoxville, Tennessee

I always like summer
best
you can eat fresh corn
from daddy's garden
and okra
and greens
and cabbage
and lots of
barbecue
and buttermilk
and homemade ice-cream
at the church picnic
and listen to
gospel music
outside
at the church
homecoming
and go to the mountains with

your grandmother

and go barefooted

and be warm

all the time

not only when you go to bed

and sleep

Nikki Giovanni

maggie and milly and
molly and may

maggie and milly and molly and may
went down to the beach(to play one day)

and maggie discovered a shell that sang
so sweetly she couldn't remember her troubles,and

milly befriended a stranded star
whose rays five languid fingers were;

and molly was chased by a horrible thing
which raced sideways while blowing bubbles:and

may came home with a smooth round stone
as small as a world and as large as alone.

For whatever we lose(like a you or a me)
it's always ourselves we find in the sea

E. E. Cummings

Louder Than a Clap of Thunder!

Louder than a clap of thunder,
louder than an eagle screams,
louder than a dragon blunders,
or a dozen football teams,
louder than a four alarmer,
or a rushing waterfall,
louder than a knight in armor
jumping from a ten-foot wall.

Louder than an earthquake rumbles,
louder than a tidal wave,
louder than an ogre grumbles
as he stumbles through his cave,
louder than stampeding cattle,
louder than a cannon roars,
louder than a giant's rattle,
that's how loud my father *SNORES!*

Jack Prelutsky

A Lesson in Manners

Someone told me someone said
You should never be bad till you've been fed.
You may, you know, be sent to bed
Without your supper.—And there you are
With nothing to eat. Not even a jar
Of pickle juice, nor a candy bar.
No, nothing to eat and nothing to drink,
And all night long to lie there and think
About washing baby's ears with ink,
Or nailing the door shut, or sassing Dad,
Or about whatever you did that was bad,
And wishing you hadn't, and feeling sad.

Now then, if what I'm told is true,
What I want to say to you—and you—
Is: MIND YOUR MANNERS. They just won't do.

If you have to be bad, you must learn to wait
Till after supper. Be good until eight.
If you let your badness come out late
It doesn't hurt to be sent to bed.
Well, not so much. So use your head:
Don't be bad till you've been fed.

John Ciardi

My Mother's Eyes

I

My mother's eyes
are cities
where birds
nest
where voyages of the ill-fated
come to rest
where the water is a mirror
of sung secrets.

II

My mother's eyes
are cities
of war
bearing the scars
of a barren time.
I approach them
and on the threshold of her eyes
a girl is rocking
asleep in a misty cruelty of light,
in windswept wastelands of absence.

In my mother's eyes
I also encounter myself
because into them
I slip,
find warm solace
and live
in the cities of love.

Marjorie Agosín

Where Have You Gone

Where have you gone

with your confident
walk with
your crooked smile

why did you leave
me
when you took your
laughter
and departed
are you aware that
with you
went the sun
all light
and what few stars
there were?

where have you gone
with your confident
walk your
crooked smile the
rent money
in one pocket and
my heart
in another . . .

Mari Evans

from In My Father's House

Always first to rise
he usually slipped into daybreak
like a phantom—heading
(in jacket jeans white socks & loafers)
for Alameda
the drowsy traffic
& buzzing electronics of Naval Air

But he plays a horn
& some mornings caught him
aching with jazz—reeling
in its chemistry & might:
Duke Bird Basie
riffs chords changes
softly grunted & mouthed
in his closet
in the hallway in
all the glory of the sunrise . . .

George Barlow

It's Windy There and Rather Weird

(Humorous Poems)

My Feet

My Feet, they haul me Round the House,
    They Hoist me up the Stairs;
I only have to Steer them, and
    They Ride me Everywheres.

Gelett Burgess

The Purple Cow

I never saw a Purple Cow,
    I never hope to see one;
But I can tell you, anyhow,
    I'd rather see than be one!

Gelett Burgess

Riddles

Which is the bow that has no arrow?
(The rainbow, that never killed a sparrow.)
Which is the singer that never had but one song?
(The cuckoo, who singeth it all day long.)

Anonymous

The land was white,
    The sea was black;
It'll take a good scholar
    To riddle that.

Anonymous

Answer: Paper and ink

In marble walls as white as milk,

Lined with a skin as soft as silk;

Within a fountain crystal clear,

A golden apple doth appear.

No doors there are to this stronghold,

Yet thieves break in and steal the gold.

Anonymous

Answer: An egg

The Germ

A mighty creature is the germ,
Though smaller than the pachyderm.
His customary dwelling place
Is deep within the human race.
His childish pride he often pleases
By giving people strange diseases.
Do you, my poppet, feel infirm?
You probably contain a germ.

Ogden Nash

My Love for You

I know you little, I love you lots;
My love for you would fill ten pots,
Fifteen buckets, sixteen cans,
Three teacups and four dishpans.

Traditional

Limericks

A diner while dining at Crewe
Found quite a large mouse in his stew.
   Said the waiter, "Don't shout,
   And wave it about,
Or the rest will be wanting one, too!"

Anonymous

There once was a young lady of Riga
   Who went out for a ride on a tiger:
   They returned from the ride
With the lady inside
And a smile on the face of the tiger.

Anonymous

Dinky

O what's the weather in a Beard?
It's windy there, and rather weird,
And when you think the sky has cleared
    —Why, there is Dirty Dinky.

Suppose you walk out in a Storm,
With nothing on to keep you warm,
And then step barefoot on a Worm,
    —Of course, it's Dirty Dinky.

As I was crossing a hot hot Plain,
I saw a sight that caused me pain,
You asked before, I'll tell you again;
    —It *looked* like Dirty Dinky.

Last night you lay a-sleeping? No!
The room was thirty-five below;
The sheets and blankets turned to snow.
    —He'd got in: Dirty Dinky.

■ You'd better watch the things you do.
■ You'd better watch the things you do.
■ You're part of him; he's part of you
    —You may be Dirty Dinky.

Theodore Roethke

Long-Leg Lou and Short-Leg Sue

Long-Leg Lou and Short-Leg Sue
Went for a walk down the avenue,
Laughin' and jokin' like good friends do,
Long-Leg Lou and Short-Leg Sue.

Says Long-Leg Lou to Short-Leg Sue,
"Can't you walk faster than you do?
It really drives me out of my mind
That I'm always in front, and you're always behind."

Says Short-Leg Sue to Long-Leg Lou,
"I walk as fast as I'm meant to do."
"Then I'll go walkin' with someone new,"
Says Long-Leg Lou to Short-Leg Sue.

Now Long-Leg Lou, he walks alone,
Looking for someone with legs like his own,
And sometimes he thinks of those warm afternoons
Back when he went walkin' with Short-Leg Sue.

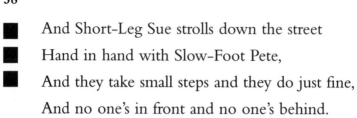

And Short-Leg Sue strolls down the street
Hand in hand with Slow-Foot Pete,
And they take small steps and they do just fine,
And no one's in front and no one's behind.

Shel Silverstein

Sing to the Sun

(The Natural World)

Song

Sing to the sun
It will listen
And warm your words
Your joy will rise
Like the sun
And glow
Within you

Sing to the moon
It will hear
And soothe your cares
Your fears will set
Like the moon
And fade
Within you

Ashley Bryan

The Sun-Dial

Every day,
Every day,
Tell the hours
By their shadows,
By their shadow.

Adelaide Crapsey

November Night

Listen.
With faint dry sound,
Like steps of passing ghosts,
The leaves, frost-crisp'd, break from the trees
And fall.

Adelaide Crapsey

The Duck

Behold the duck.
It does not cluck.
A cluck it lacks.
It quacks.
It is specially fond
Of a puddle or pond.
When it dines or sups,
It bottoms ups.

Ogden Nash

◼ Fog
◼
◼

The fog comes
on little cat feet.

It sits looking
over harbor and city
on silent haunches
and then moves on.

Carl Sandburg

Voices That Beautify the Earth

Voice above,
Voice of Thunder;
Speak from the dark of clouds;
Voice below,
Grasshopper-voice,
Speak from the green of plants;
So may the earth be beautiful.

Cherokee

Swift Things Are Beautiful

Swift things are beautiful:
Swallows and deer,
And lightning that falls
Bright-veined and clear,
Rivers and meteors,
Wind in the wheat,
The strong-withered horse,
The runner's sure feet.

And slow things are beautiful:
The closing of day,
The pause of a wave
That curves downward to spray,
The ember that crumbles,
The opening flower,
And the ox that moves on
In the quiet of power.

Elizabeth Coatsworth

the earth is a living thing

is a black shuffling bear
ruffling its wild back and tossing
mountains into the sea

is a black hawk circling
the burying ground circling the bones
picked clean and discarded

is a fish black blind in the belly of water
is a diamond blind in the black belly of coal

is a black and living thing
is a favorite child
of the universe
feel her rolling her hand
in its kinky hair
feel her brushing it clean

Lucille Clifton

■ Dusk
■
■

swifts and swallows
Snapping up insects
swifts and swallows.

Barn swallows
swifts and swallows
Cliff swallows
cave swallows
swifts and swallows

swallows
swift swallows
swift swallows

swift swallows
swift swallows
swift swallows

At dusk there are swallows
swifts and swallows

swifts and swallows.
Barn swallows
bank swallows
swifts and swallows

Cliff swallows
swifts and swallows
Swift and all-swallowing
swallows

swift swallows
swift swallows
swift swallows
swift swallows
swift swallows

Paul Fleischman

Counting-out Rhyme

Silver bark of beech, and sallow
Bark of yellow birch and yellow
    Twig of willow.

Stripe of green in moosewood maple,
Color seen in leaf of apple,
    Bark of popple.

Wood of popple pale as moonbeam,
Wood of oak for yoke and barn-beam,
    Wood of hornbeam.

Silver bark of beech, and hollow
Stem of elder, tall and yellow
    Twig of willow.

Edna St. Vincent Millay

The Delight Song of Tsoai-talee

I am a feather on the bright sky
I am the blue horse that runs in the plain
I am the fish that rolls, shining, in the water
I am the shadow that follows a child
I am the evening light, the lustre of meadows
I am an eagle playing with the wind
I am a cluster of bright beads
I am the farthest star
I am the cold of the dawn
I am the roaring of the rain
I am the glitter on the crust of the snow
I am the long track of the moon in a lake
I am a flame of four colors
I am a deer standing away in the dusk
I am a field of sumac and the pomme blanche
I am an angle of geese in the winter sky
I am the hunger of a young wolf
I am the whole dream of these things

You see, I am alive, I am alive

I stand in good relation to the earth

I stand in good relation to the gods

I stand in good relation to all that is beautiful

I stand in good relation to the daughter of Tsen-tainte

You see, I am alive, I am alive

N. Scott Momaday

Zanzibar and Timbuktu and Lollipagowe

(Wisdom and Wonder)

What Are Heavy

What are heavy? Sea-sand and sorrow.

What are brief? Today and tomorrow.

What are frail? Spring blossoms and youth.

What are deep? The ocean and truth.

Christina Rossetti

O To Be a Dragon

If I, like Solomon, . . .
could have my wish—

my wish . . . O to be a dragon,
a symbol of the power of Heaven—of silkworm
size or immense; at times invisible.
Felicitous phenomenon!

Marianne Moore

The Jewel

There is this cave
In the air behind my body
That nobody is going to touch:
A cloister, a silence
Closing around a blossom of fire.
When I stand upright in the wind,
My bones turn to dark emeralds.

James Wright

from **A Birthday**

My heart is like a singing bird
    Whose nest is in a watered shoot;
My heart is like an apple tree
    Whose boughs are bent with thickset fruit;
My heart is like a rainbow shell
    That paddles on a halcyon sea;
My heart is gladder than all these
    Because my love is come to me.

Christina Rossetti

halcyon = calm, peaceful

■ I Saw a Peacock
■
■

I saw a Peacock with a fiery tail,

I saw a blazing Comet drop down hail,

I saw a Cloud with ivy circled round,

I saw a sturdy Oak creep on the ground,

I saw a Pismire swallow up a whale,

I saw a raging Sea brim full of ale,

I saw a Venice Glass sixteen foot deep,

I saw a Well full of men's tears that weep,

I saw their Eyes all in a flame of fire,

I saw a House as big as the moon and higher,

I saw the Sun even in the midst of night,

I saw the Man that saw this wondrous sight.

Traditional

Pismire = ant

The Word Woman

I met an old lady,
I met her on the stair,
Her apron was of silver,
And silver was her hair.
Her arms were piled high with ephemeral things,
And I think (now that I think of it), she almost had wings.

Though her arms were laden,
She walked without a care,
A little silver lady on an old wooden stair.
Her hair was in a top-knot, tied with a bow,
And she wore a dappled shawl
And her dress, just so.
I asked what she carried,
What she carried up the stair,
And she looked at me and laughed a laugh that matched
    her silver hair.

"I carry words," she said to me,
"I keep them in a jar,
And some of them," she whispered,
"Have come quite far.
There's Zanzibar and Timbuktu and Lollipagowe,
Agawam and Rippowam and Timboome.

I keep them in the attic in a clear glass jar
And when I feel like traveling
I thread one to a star.
Words like 'soap' and 'bubbly' I pile in my sink,
Words like 'far' and 'lovely', let me think—"
She cocked her head and gazed at me
And then she was no more—
All I saw was silver,
streaked across the floor.

Patricia Hubbell

The Naming of Cats

The Naming of Cats is a difficult matter,
    It isn't just one of your holiday games;
You may think at first I'm mad as a hatter
When I tell you, a cat must have THREE DIFFERENT NAMES.
First of all, there's the name that the family use daily,
    Such as Peter, Augustus, Alonzo or James,
Such as Victor or Jonathan, George or Bill Bailey—
    All of them sensible everyday names.
There are fancier names if you think they sound sweeter,
    Some for the gentlemen, some for the dames:
Such as Plato, Admetus, Electra, Demeter—
    But all of them sensible everyday names.
But I tell you, a cat needs a name that's particular,
    A name that's peculiar and more dignified,
Else how can he keep up his tail perpendicular,
    Or spread out his whiskers, or cherish his pride?
Of names of this kind, I can give you a quorum,
    Such as Munkustrap, Quaxo, or Coricopat,

Such as Bombalurina, or else Jellylorum—
    Names that never belong to more than one cat.
But above and beyond there's still one name left over,
    And that is the name that you never will guess;
The name that no human research can discover—
    BUT THE CAT HIMSELF KNOWS, and will never confess.

T. S. Eliot

The Owl and the Pussy-Cat

The Owl and the Pussy-cat went to sea
    In a beautiful pea-green boat,
They took some honey, and plenty of money,
    Wrapped up in a five-pound note.
The Owl looked up to the stars above,
    And sang to a small guitar,
"O lovely Pussy, O Pussy, my love,
    What a beautiful Pussy you are,
        You are,
        You are!
    What a beautiful Pussy you are!"

Pussy said to the Owl, "You elegant fowl,
    How charmingly sweet you sing!
O let us be married; too long we have tarried:
    But what shall we do for a ring?"
They sailed away, for a year and a day,
    To the land where the Bong-tree grows;

And there in a wood a Piggy-wig stood,
    With a ring at the end of his nose,
        His nose,
        His nose,
    With a ring at the end of his nose.

"Dear Pig, are you willing to sell for one shilling
    Your ring?" Said the Piggy, "I will."
So they took it away, and were married next day
    By the Turkey who lives on the hill.
They dined on mince and slices of quince,
    Which they ate with a runcible spoon;
And hand in hand, on the edge of the sand,
    They danced by the light of the moon,
        The moon,
        The moon,
    They danced by the light of the moon.

Edward Lear

Casabianca

[Casabianca, a brave and dedicated boy about thirteen years old, son of the admiral, kept his post during the Battle of the Nile, even after the ship caught on fire, and all others had abandoned ship. Casabianca died when the ship exploded.]

The boy stood on the burning deck,
  Whence all but him had fled;
The flame that lit the battle's wreck
  Shone round him o'er the dead.

Yet beautiful and bright he stood,
  As born to rule the storm;
A creature of heroic blood,
  A proud though childlike form.

The flames rolled on; he would not go
  Without his father's word;
That father, faint in death below,
  His voice no longer heard.

He called aloud, "Say, father, say,
    If yet my task be done?"
He knew not that the chieftain lay
    Unconscious of his son.

"Speak, father!" once again he cried,
    "If I may yet be gone!"
And but the booming shots replied,
    And fast the flames rolled on.

Upon his brow he felt their breath,
    And in his waving hair,
And looked from that lone post of death
    In still yet brave despair;

And shouted but once more aloud,
    "My father! must I stay?"
While o'er him fast, through sail and shroud,
    The wreathing fires made way.

They wrapt the ship in splendor wild,
    They caught the flag on high,
And streamed above the gallant child,
    Like banners in the sky.

There came a burst of thunder sound;
    The boy,—Oh! where was he?
Ask of the winds, that far around
    With fragments strewed the sea,—

With shroud and mast and pennon fair,
    That well had borne their part,—
But the noblest thing that perished there
    Was that young, faithful heart.

Felicia Hemans

Resources

The following biographical notes and selected works for further reading provide a good starting place for teachers, parents, or young readers who want to know more about some of the authors whose poems appear in *Whisper and Shout*. Among the works suggested are collections of poetry and, in some cases, biographies of the poets, or works they've written about writing. While many of these books were written for adults, some are children's books, and this is indicated after the title. As a teacher, when I'm looking for new poetry to bring to students, I scan lots of poems to get to the just-right ones that I think will speak to a particular group of kids. All the poets in this book have other work appropriate for fourth- to sixth-grade students as well; but you may need to look closely through some collections to find the ones that work best.

In addition to the books by and about the poets in this volume included below, two additional titles will support you in discovering more about the mechanics of poetry, what makes a poem a poem, and in learning about all kinds of poetry: *The Making of a Poem: A Norton Anthology of Poetic Forms,* edited by Mark Strand and Eavan Boland (Norton, 2000), and *The Sounds of Poetry: A Brief Guide,* by Robert Pinsky (Farrar, Straus and Giroux, 1998).

Marjorie Agosín (b. 1955) is a professor of Spanish at Wellesley College, where she teaches courses in Spanish language and Latin American literature. She received the 1995 Letras de Oro prize for poetry; and the Latino Literature Prize for poetry, awarded by the Latin American Writers Institute for her book *Toward the Splendid City.* Agosín is a well-known spokesperson for the plight and priorities of women in Third World countries.

SUGGESTED READING

 The Alphabet in My Hands: A Writing Life, translated by Nancy Abraham (Rutger's University Press).

 A Cross and a Star: Memoirs of a Jewish Girl in Chile (Feminist Press).

 Starry Night: Poems (White Pine Press).

Born in Berkeley, California, **George Barlow** (b. 1948) received an M.F.A. from the University of Iowa Writers' Workshop in 1972 and is currently associate professor of American studies and English at Grinnell College. He is the author of two books of poetry: *Gumbo,* a National Poetry Series selection; and *Gabriel.* His poetry has appeared in a number of literary magazines and anthologies, including *Every Shut Eye Ain't Asleep: An Anthology of Poetry by African Americans since 1945,* and *Motion: American Sports Poetry.*

SUGGESTED READING

Gabriel (Broadside Press). Poetry.

African American writer **Gwendolyn Brooks** (1917–2000) was best known for her poetry, which won her the Pulitzer Prize in 1950. She also wrote novels and short stories. She lived in Chicago, where she was a professor at Chicago State University, and contributed reviews to major newspapers. Early in her career, she worked as publicity director for the National Association for the Advancement of Colored People.

SUGGESTED READING

A Life of Gwendolyn Brooks, by George E. Kent (University Press of Kentucky).

Selected Poems (HarperCollins).

Best known as an author and illustrator of children's books, **Ashley Bryan** (b. 1923) is a poet with a large, resonant voice, whose reading of his poems brings them vibrantly to life. His work as a folklorist has brought an awareness and appreciation of traditional black spirituals to many children and adults. He is now professor emeritus of Dartmouth College, where he taught art.

SUGGESTED READING

Ashley Bryan's ABC's of African American Poetry (Atheneum). Children's poetry.

Ashley Bryan's African Tales, Uh-Huh (Atheneum). Children's folktales.

Jump Back, Honey: The Poems of Paul Dunbar (Hyperion). Children's poetry.

American humorist and writer **Gelett Burgess** (1866–1951) wrote stories, plays, and poems, and was most admired for his novels, primarily suspenseful fiction.

SUGGESTED READING

Goops and How to Be Them: A Manual of Manners for Polite Infants Inculcating Many Juvenile Virtues Both by Precept and Example, with 90 Drawings (Dover Publications). Children's poetry.

English writer **Lewis Carroll** (1832–1898) is known to the world as the author of *Alice's Adventures in Wonderland,* a book that is now a classic of children's literature. It was first published in 1865. "Lewis Carroll" is the pseudonym for Rev. Charles Lutwidge Dodgson, a mathematics lecturer at Oxford University.

SUGGESTED READING

> *Humorous Verses of Lewis Carroll* (Dover). Children's poetry.
> *Lewis Carroll: Poetry for Young People* (Sterling). Children's poetry.

John Ciardi (1916–1986) wrote poetry for adults and children, as well as literary criticism, history, and translations. Ciardi taught at several universities, including Harvard and Rutgers. Of his interests outside of writing, he said he enjoyed "indifferent golf and neglected gardening."

SUGGESTED READING

> *The Collected Poems of John Ciardi* (University of Arkansas Press).
> *Doodle Soup* (Houghton Mifflin). Children's poetry.

The poems of **Lucille Clifton** (b. 1936) were first published in a poetry anthology by Langston Hughes. The first person in her family to finish high school and enter college, Clifton attended Howard University. Twice nominated for the Pulitzer Prize, Clifton is the author of more than sixteen children's books, including her Everett Anderson series. She currently lives in Maryland.

SUGGESTED READING

> *Good Woman: Poems and a Memoir 1969–1980* (BOA Editions, Ltd).
>
> *The Book of Light* (BOA Editions, Ltd). Poetry.

Elizabeth Coatsworth (1893–1986) is best known for her 1931 Newbery Medal–winning children's novel, *The Cat Who Went to Heaven*. As a girl, with her family, Coatsworth visited the Alps, traveled across the Egyptian deserts, and hiked in Yosemite. After she received her master's degree, she spent over a year in the Far East. A prolific writer for both adults and young people, Coatsworth wrote over ninety books of fiction and poetry for children.

SUGGESTED READING

> *The Cat Who Went to Heaven* (Simon & Schuster). Children's fiction.
>
> *Poems* (MacMillan, o.p.).

Poet and performance artist ***Jayne Cortez*** (b. 1935) is the author of ten books and has performed her poetry, set to music, on several recordings. She can be seen in the films *Women in Jazz* and *Poetry in Motion,* and is the cofounder of the Watts Repertory Theatre Company. Her awards include an American Book Award and a creative writing fellowship from the National Endowment for the Arts. Cortez has read her poetry in the United States, Europe, Africa, Latin America, and the Caribbean.

SUGGESTED READING

> *Coagulations: New and Selected Poems* (Thunder Mouth Press).
>
> *Somewhere in Advance of Nowhere* (Serpent's Tail Books). Poetry.

Adelaide Crapsey (1878–1914) was born in New York and died of tuberculosis when she was only thirty-six years old. Crapsey, who taught poetry at Smith College, is best known as the inventor of the cinquain, a form of poetry based on five-line stanzas. During her lifetime she compiled only one volume of her poetry, which was published after her death.

SUGGESTED READING

> *Complete Poems and Collected Letters of Adelaide Crapsey,* edited by Susan Sutton Smith (State University of New York Press).

E. E. Cummings (1894–1962) was born in Massachusetts, and received his B.A. and M.A. from Harvard. During World War I, Cummings served as an ambulance driver in France, but was interned in a prison camp by the French authorities for speaking out in opposition to the war. He later wrote about this experience in his novel *The Enormous Room*. Cummings is known for his inventive use of form, punctuation, spelling, and syntax to create a very original style of poetry.

SUGGESTED READING

E. E. Cummings: Complete Poems, 1904–1962 (Livright).

Hist, Whist, illustrated by Deborah Kogan Ray (Crown). Children's poetry.

During her lifetime *Emily Dickinson* (1830–1886) published only ten poems, and yet her work, along with Walt Whitman's, drastically changed the direction of American poetry, giving it more stylistic range and poetic freedom. Dickinson lived a solitary life, rarely leaving home. After her death, 1,700 poems on scraps of paper, some of which she'd bound into booklets, were discovered, and some of her poems were then published in a heavily edited form. It wasn't until 1955, however, that her poetry appeared in print as she had written it.

SUGGESTED READING

The Complete Poems of Emily Dickinson, edited by Thomas H. Johnson (Little, Brown).

The Life of Emily Dickinson, by Richard B. Sewall (Harvard University Press).

T. S. Eliot (1888–1965) was born in St. Louis, Missouri, and moved to England in 1927. After earning both undergraduate and graduate degrees from the Sorbonne in Paris, Eliot taught at grammar schools in London and then became a bank clerk. He lectured at Trinity College, London, and later taught at Harvard University. Considered to be a major figure in modern American poetry, he received the 1948 Nobel Prize for Literature. *Old Possum's Book of Practical Cats,* a book of fourteen rhymes, was the inspiration for the musical *Cats.*

SUGGESTED READING

Collected Poems, 1909–1962 (Harcourt).

Old Possum's Book of Practical Cats, illustrated by Edward Gorey (Harcourt). Poetry.

Mari Evans, an educator, writer, and musician, resides in Indianapolis. She formerly held the post of distinguished writer and professor at Cornell University, and has taught at a number of prestigious universities over the past twenty years. She is the author of four children's books, several theater pieces that have been performed, two musical plays, and four volumes of poetry. Evans edited the highly acclaimed *Black Women Writers (1950–1980): A Critical Evaluation*. Much of her work is familiar to young readers, as it has been anthologized in over 400 poetry collections and textbooks.

SUGGESTED READING

A Dark and Splendid Mass (Writers and Readers). Poetry.
Dear Corinne, Tell Somebody! Love, Annie: A Book about Secrets (Just Us Books). Children's fiction.

Author of many books for young readers, **Paul Fleischman** (b. 1952) has won both a Newbery Medal and a Newbery Honor. In addition to being a fiction writer, Fleischman is a musician, poet, found-object sculptor, and founder of a troupe of adults and children who perform stories illustrated with string figures. A native Californian, Fleischman makes his home in Monterey.

SUGGESTED READING

I Am a Phoenix: Poems for Two Voices, illustrated by Ken Nutt (HarperCollins). Children's poetry.

Joyful Noise: Poems for Two Voices, illustrated by Eric Beddows (HarperCollins). Children's poetry.

Though **Robert Frost** (1874–1963) attended college, he never earned a formal degree. After leaving school, he worked as a teacher, cobbler, and editor. Frost had begun writing poetry when he was in high school, and by the 1920s was the most celebrated poet in the United States: in 1961, he read one of his poems at the inauguration of President Kennedy. Much of his poetry, written in traditional verse forms, is about the life and landscape of New England. Frost taught poetry at universities for many years.

SUGGESTED READING

Robert Frost: A Life, by Jay Parini (Henry Holt).

Robert Frost: Collected Poems, Prose, and Plays, edited by Mark Richardson and Richard Poirier (Library of America).

Nikki Giovanni (b. 1943) was born in Knoxville, Tennessee, and raised in Ohio. As a student at Fisk University, she edited the school's literary magazine. Giovanni's first book was published when she was in her early twenties. Much of her work reflects on the African American identity. In 1989 the National Association for the Advancement of Colored People named her woman of the year. She is currently a professor of black studies at Virginia Tech.

SUGGESTED READING

The Selected Poems of Nikki Giovanni (Morrow).

Spin a Soft Black Song (Hill & Wang). Children's poetry.

English poet **Felicia Hemans**'s (1793–1835) first book of poems was published when she was just fourteen years old. From childhood, she had the remarkable ability to recite long poems after having read them only once. A best-selling poet in England and America, and an important literary figure of the early nineteenth century, Felicia Hemans was regarded as a leading woman poet in her day.

SUGGESTED READING

Records of Women, with Other Poems, edited by Paula R. Feldman (University Press of Kentucky).

Children's author **Patricia Hubbell** (b. 1928) has been writing poetry since she was eleven years old. In 1998, she received the *Parents Magazine* Book of the Year Award for her book *Wrapping Paper Romp.* Hubbell lives with her husband in Easton, Connecticut, the small town where she was born.

> *Boo! Halloween Poems and Limericks,* illustrated by Jeff Spackman (Marshall Cavendish). Children's poetry.
>
> *City Kids: Poems,* illustrated by Teresa Flavin (Marshall Cavendish). Children's poetry.

Langston Hughes (1902–1967) was born in Missouri. His parents divorced when he was young, and he was raised by his grandmother until he was twelve, when he went to live with his mother. Hughes began writing poems when he was in high school. In 1924 he moved to Harlem, New York. His first book of poems came out when he was twenty-four, and he graduated from college three years later. His poetry is known for its portrayals of African American life. In addition to poems, he wrote novels, short stories, plays, and books for children. Jazz, a form of music with roots in the African American experience, had a strong influence on his work.

SUGGESTED READING

> *The Book of Rhythms,* with introduction by Wynton Marsalis (Oxford University Press). Children's nonfiction.
>
> *The Collected Poems of Langston Hughes,* edited by Arnold Rampersad (Vintage Classics).

Edward Lear (1812–1888) was born in England. His parents' twentieth child, he was raised, to a great extent, by an older sister. In 1826 he began to earn a living as an artist and first became known as an ornithological draftsman. As a young man, he described himself by saying "Both my knees are fractured from being run over, which has made them very peculiarly crooked . . . my neck is singularly long, [I have] a most elephantine nose—and a disposition to tumble here and there. . . ." Lear traveled extensively in Europe, as well as to Egypt and Greece. His first picture book was published in 1851.

SUGGESTED READING

A Book of Nonsense (Knopf). Children's poetry.

An Edward Lear Alphabet, illustrated by Vladimir Radunsky (HarperCollins). Children's poetry.

When *Herman Melville* (1819–1891) died, a newspaper obituary stated that he had been long forgotten, and was likely unknown to the readers of the paper. Now, however, his book *Moby Dick,* the story of a whaling ship and an invincible white whale, published forty years before his death, is considered a classic work. Melville was the author of many books but published little during the last thirty years of his life when he worked as a clerk in the New York custom-house. Melville had an interesting appearance—"a great growth of hair and beard, and a keen blue eye."

SUGGESTED READING

Moby Dick (Bantam). Fiction.

The Poems of Herman Melville, edited by Douglas Robillard (Kent State University Press).

Edna St. Vincent Millay's (1892–1950) mother raised her four daughters on her own, encouraging her girls to be ambitious and self-sufficient. At the age of twenty, Millay won a poetry prize that brought her immediate acclaim and a scholarship to Vassar College. Her first book of poems appeared in 1917. After college she lived in Greenwich Village, in New York City. She later moved to Maine. During much of her career, Millay, a Pulitzer Prize–winner, was one of the most successful and respected poets in America. In addition to writing poetry, Millay wrote plays.

SUGGESTED READING

Savage Beauty: The Life of Edna St. Vincent Millay, by Nancy Milford (Random).

The Selected Poems of Edna St. Vincent Millay, edited by Nancy Milford (Modern Library).

N. Scott Momaday (b. 1934) writes novels, short stories, poetry, and memoirs. He received his M.A. from Stanford University. His work celebrates his Native American heritage, as his father was Kiowa and his mother, the descendant of early American pioneers, had a great-grandmother who was Cherokee. Momaday, who was awarded the Pulitzer Prize for fiction in 1969, has taught at several universities.

SUGGESTED READING

> *In the Presence of the Sun: Stories and Poems* (St. Martin's Press).
>
> *The Man Made of Words: Essays, Stories, Passages* (Griffin).

Marianne Moore (1887–1972) was born in Missouri and raised in the home of her grandfather. She graduated from Bryn Mawr College in 1909. Moore worked as a teacher at the Carlisle Indian School, and moved to New York City in 1918, where she became an assistant at the New York Public Library. Moore's many honors include the National Book Award and the Pulitzer Prize. She cared deeply about animals, and her poetry was inspired by nature. She was also a great fan of baseball and an admirer of Muhammad Ali.

SUGGESTED READING

> *Complete Poems* (Penguin).
>
> *Marianne Moore: A Literary Life,* by Charles Molesworth (Northeastern University Press).

Ogden Nash (1902–1971) was a prolific writer, whose work includes poetry for children and adults, children's fiction, plays, and screenplays. He is most famous for his humorous, quotable verses. He published his first children's book when he was twenty-three, and his first poem appeared in print in *The New Yorker* in 1930, a magazine whose staff he later joined.

SUGGESTED READING

> *The Tale of Custard the Dragon,* illustrated by Lynn Munsinger (Little, Brown). Children's poetry.

Brooklyn-born children's book author **Jack Prelutsky** (b. 1940) claims to have hated poetry through most of his childhood. After working as a truckdriver, photographer, folksinger, and more, Prelutsky turned to writing. He has more than thirty collections of original verse and anthologies of children's poetry to his name. Prelutsky lives with his wife, Carolyn, in Washington State.

SUGGESTED READING

> *Awful Ogre's Awful Day: Poems,* illustrated by Paul O. Zelinsky (Greenwillow). Children's poetry.
>
> *A Pizza the Size of the Sun: Poems,* illustrated by James Stevenson (Greenwillow). Children's poetry.

Theodore Roethke (1908–1963) was born in Michigan. As a child, he spent a great deal of time in the greenhouse

105

owned by his father and uncle. Later, the natural world he witnessed as a child strongly influenced his poetry. Roethke went to college, but wasn't happy there. He later taught at various colleges and universities. His first book of poems took ten years to write and was highly regarded when it was published. In 1954 he was awarded the Pulitzer Prize.

SUGGESTED READING

The Complete Poems (Penguin Classics).

The Glass House: The Life of Theodore Roethke, by Allan Seager (University of Michigan Press).

Born in London, ***Christina Rossetti*** (1830–1894) was one of the most significant woman poets writing in nineteenth-century England. A devout member of the evangelical branch of the Church of England, Rossetti lived a secluded life.

SUGGESTED READING

Christina Rossetti, by Kathryn Burlison (University Press of Mississippi). Biography.

The Complete Poems (Penguin Classics).

Carl Sandburg (1878–1967) was born in Illinois. At thirteen, Sandburg left school to help support his family; at seventeen, he fought in Puerto Rico during the Spanish-American War. In college, a professor so admired Sandburg's poetry that he paid for its publication. Sandburg worked at many jobs, including stints as a milk-delivery boy, fireman, and newspaper reporter, then became an editorial writer. In addition to writing poetry, he devoted himself to a study of Abraham Lincoln. Much of Sandburg's work is a celebration of America.

SUGGESTED READING

Carl Sandburg: A Biography, by Milton Meltzer (Twenty-First Century Books).

The Complete Poems of Carl Sandburg (Harcourt Brace).

Poetry for Young People: Carl Sandburg (Sterling). Children's poetry.

William Shakespeare (c. 1564) is the world's most famous and respected playwright. He was born in England to middle-class parents and wrote more than thirty plays, which were performed in the famous Globe Theater. The sonnets that Shakespeare wrote consisted of three quatrains (four-line stanzas) and a couplet (a two-line stanza), a form now known as the Shakespearean sonnet.

SUGGESTED READING

Complete Poems of Shakespeare (Random House).

Shel Silverstein (1932–1999) was born in Chicago, Illinois, and began writing when he was a young boy. In addition to writing for young people, he was a composer and an artist. He illustrated his own picture books, which include such favorites as *The Giving Tree* and *The Missing Piece Meets the Big O.*

SUGGESTED READING

A Light in the Attic (HarperCollins). Children's poetry.

Where the Sidewalk Ends (HarperCollins). Children's poetry.

May Swenson (1919–1989), the author of many books of poems, grew up in Utah and received her B.A. from Utah State University. She taught poetry at several universities and gave readings of her work at over fifty universities. Swenson received much acclaim for her writing and was the recipient of a MacArthur Fellowship. Her poems are surprising in their use of wordplay and for the distinctive ways they appear on the page.

SUGGESTED READING

The Complete Poems to Solve, illustrated by Christy Hale (Macmillan). Children's poetry.

Nature: Poems Old and New (Houghton Mifflin).

Born in Pennsylvania, **John Updike** (b. 1932) is a poet, essayist, short-story writer, and novelist. One of America's most distinguished and prolific writers, Updike has received numerous honors and awards, including the National Book Award and two Pulitzer Prizes. His picture book, illustrated by Trina Schart Hyman, *A Child's Calendar,* was a 2000 Caldecott Honor Book. Updike now lives in Massachusetts.

SUGGESTED READING

A Child's Calendar, illustrated by Trina Schart Hyman (Holiday House). Children's poetry.

Collected Poems: 1953–1993 (Knopf).

Walt Whitman (1819–1892) learned the printer's trade when he was twelve, was largely self-taught, and loved to read. Whitman worked as a printer and taught in one-room schoolhouses on Long Island, New York. Later, he became a journalist, and in 1855 he self-published his book *Leaves of Grass,* considered one of the world's major literary works. Whitman's free-verse poetry with its innovative rhythms was surprising at a time when most poetry was written using strict rhyme schemes.

SUGGESTED READING

> *Walt Whitman: The Complete Poems,* edited by Francis
> Murphy (Viking).
>
> *Walt Whitman's America: A Cultural Biography,* by David S.
> Reynold (Vintage).

James Wright (1927–1980) was born in Ohio. When he graduated from high school in 1946 he joined the army and was stationed in Japan during the American occupation. He graduated from Kenyon College, later received his doctorate, and taught at several universities. Wright's poetry was greatly influenced by the poverty and human suffering that he witnessed as a child. His earlier work is written in conventional poetic meter, while his later poems display a more open style. The Pulitzer Prize was awarded to him for his *Collected Poems.*

SUGGESTED READING

> *The Branch Will Not Break* (Wesleyan University Press).
> Poetry.
>
> *Above the River: The Collected Poems* (Noonday Press).

Cynthia Zarin (b. 1959) is from New York City, and is the author of six books—two collections of poetry and four picture books. She has worked as a staff writer for *The New*

Yorker magazine, taught creative writing at universities, and served as an artist-in-residence at the Cathedral of St. John the Divine in New York.

SUGGESTED READING

The Water Course: Poems (Knopf).

What Do You See When You Shut Your Eyes?, illustrated by Sarah Durham (Houghton Mifflin). Children's poetry.

Permissions

Permission for use of the following is gratefully acknowledged. Every effort has been made to contact copyright owners. In the event of an omission, please notify the publishers of this volume so that corrections can be made in future editions.

"My Mother's Eyes" by Marjorie Agosín. Copyright © 2002 by Marjorie Agosín. Reprinted by permission of the author.

"In My Father's House" by George Barlow. Copyright © 1981 by George Barlow. Reprinted by permission of the author.

"Speech to the Young: Speech to the Progress-Toward" by Gwendolyn Brooks from *Blacks*. Copyright © 1987 by Gwendolyn Brooks. Reprinted by permission of the estate of Gwendolyn Brooks.

"Song" by Ashley Bryan. Copyright © 1992 by Ashley Bryan. Reprinted by permission of HarperCollins Publishers.

"A Lesson in Manners" by John Ciardi from *Doodle Soup* by John Ciardi. Copyright © 1985 by Myra J. Ciardi. Reprinted by permission of Houghton Mifflin Company. All rights reserved.

"the earth is a living thing" by Lucille Clifton from *The Book of Light*. Copyright © 1993 by Lucille Clifton. Reprinted by permission

114

Index of Titles

117

Index of First Lines

Index of Authors